AN ILLUSTRATED GUIDE TO THE BURIED CITIES OF CEYLON

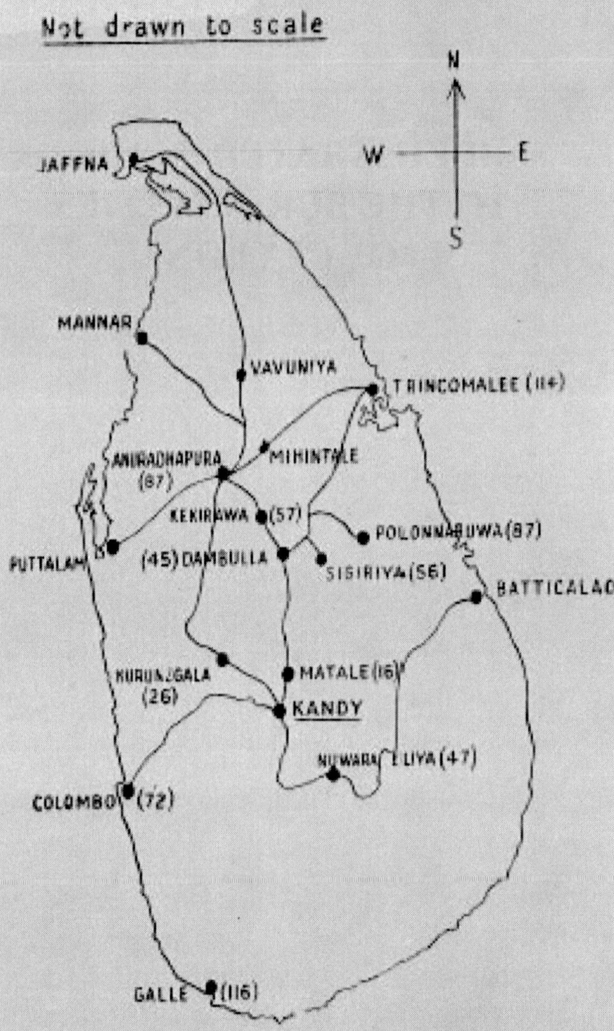

MAP OF CEYLON

Shewing positions of places mentioned in Guide Book

Numbers denote Miles from KANDY

AN ILLUSTRATED GUIDE TO THE BURIED CITIES OF CEYLON

JONES-BATEMAN

GYAN

Published by

GYAN

Gyan Publishing House
5, Ansari Road
Daryaganj, New Delhi-110002
Phone: 011-47034999, 9811692060
E-mail: books@gyanbooks.com

Distribution Network
gyanbooks.com
India, USA, Canada, UK, Australia, France

ISBN : 978-81-212-3563-1 (PB)
First Published, Kandy, 1932

2nd Impression 2020

Printed at: Gyan Press, Delhi.

An
Illustrated Guide to the Buried Cities of Ceylon
Author: Jones-Bateman

CONTENTS

LIST OF ILLUSTRATIONS

FACING PAGE

LIST OF ILLUSTRATIONS

MAPS

PREFACE

CEYLON is becoming increasingly popular with tourists, and many of our very welcome visitors endeavour to see something of the Buried Cities. These lie amid the jungles of the northern plains somewhat removed from the civilisation of Colombo and Kandy. The result of a hurried visit is invariably a bad attack of 'antique indigestion'. This small guide to the ruins is intended to give the traveller an opportunity of acquiring the main historical and archæological facts at his leisure.

For the greater part of the year the climate of the Buried Cities is uncomfortably hot. The rainfall of Anuradhapura is some fifty inches per annum, but most of this falls during the north-east monsoon between October and January, known locally as the fever season. The latter half of January is the best time for a visit. The climate is then cool, the tanks are full of water, and the old grey stones have a fitting setting amid the green grass of the parklands. The great rain trees spread a generous shade, and paddy fields and palm groves are full of life. From the end of January there is a crescendo of heat. It is a dry heat, not as trying as the damp heat of Colombo, but even the acclimatised find it difficult to muster much energy wherewith to climb dagabas. There is 'some soul of goodness' in this evil, for we owe the preservation of the ruins to the lack of humidity in the atmosphere.

The visitor will need good sun-glasses and a topee or double terai which has utilitarian rather than ornamental features. Strong walking-shoes are essential, and the female will be well advised to abandon sleeveless frocks for the time being. Malaria has played no small part in the history of the Sinhalese, and shares with Tamil invaders from Southern India the responsibility for the abandonment of the cities of the plains. The anopheles mosquito continues to flourish in spite of an intensive anti-malarial campaign, and five grains of quinine every day or so is advisable, if not essential. Drinking-water north of Matale, unless boiled and filtered, should be avoided. It can be improved for ablutionary purposes by the addition of a few drops of Scrubb's Ammonia, which is a most effective weapon for dealing with insect bites.

Anuradhapura boasts an excellent hotel, well equipped and most efficiently run. At Polonnaruwa and Sigiriya the visitor perforce seeks accommodation in the Rest House. This is a Government institution with the requisite furniture, crockery, and linen. The last-named commodity was bought for durability, and the fastidious should take their own. Beds, of course, are occupied by all and sundry. On circuit in my husband's old jungle district north of Anuradhapura I once attempted to occupy a bed in a very primitive Rest House. It was found on inspection to contain a goat. Under this quadruped were three hens' eggs, and needless to say the population did not end at that. Let me hasten to state that the beds at the Rest Houses on the beaten track are reasonably clean and comfortable. The Rest House keeper is supposed to supply necessary meals, and when he happens to be anything of a shikari his larder will contain fresh meat and game. Fruit, of course, grows everywhere, and fish from the village tank is by no means to be despised.

Photographers will find the atmosphere of the Buried Cities difficult. There is plenty of sunlight, but the best results are obtained when there is a minimum of shadow, which is unfortunately the hottest time of day. Negatives are apt to be fogged for no apparent reason, and after some years' experience with a camera among the ruins I have come to the conclusion that one must sacrifice comfort for clear-cut negatives.

It remains but to state the sources from which the materials of this book have been derived. Chief among these is the old Buddhist chronicle, the Mahawansa, and its sequel, the Cūlamvaṁsa. This history of the great kings of the Lion Race was written in Pali in the 5th century A.D. by a monk Mahanama, "for the serene joy and emotion of the pious." Quotations, unless otherwise stated, are from Geiger's translation. Parker's *Ancient Ceylon* has been invaluable in the matter of history and construction, and I can recommend Smither's *Architectural Survey of the Ruins of Anuradhapura* to those interested in details of carving. Dates at the very early period are of necessity almost a matter of conjecture. They are further complicated by the effort of Mahanama to make the landing of the first Sinhalese, Vijaya, coincide with the year of Buddha's death. Mr. Codrington in his excellent *Short History of Ceylon* has reduced things to some kind of chronological order, and I have followed such an expert with no misgivings.

I am greatly indebted to my husband and many friends who have suffered so much from my "bump of antiquity." Finally, much is due to that eminent scholar Dr. Andreas Nell, under whose expert guidance I first trod the paths of archæology. His gift of a Madara stick and a vaedda charm wherewith to ward off the attacks of wild elephants and snake-bite has no doubt made the rifles of my companions unnecessary.

DOROTHY JONES-BATEMAN.

KANDY, 1932.

GUARD STONES AND STEPS NEAR BASAWAK-KULAM, ANURADHAPURA

THE BURIED CITIES

THE history of the Sinhalese in Ceylon begins with the coming of Vijaya in the 6th century B.C. His grandmother, a princess of Bengal, ran away from home and mated with a lion (*sinha*) ; hence we have the Sinhalese or Lion Race. Vijaya conquered the island aided by Kuweni, a Yakkhini, one of the original inhabitants. Discarded by Vijaya, she and her two children wander into the interior. Kuweni is slain by her relatives and the children find refuge in the Adam's Peak district to become the ancestors of the Vaeddas. This primitive people still exists in rapidly decreasing numbers in the more remote jungles of Ceylon.

In the early part of the 5th century B.C. the grandson of Vijaya's nephew takes over the town of Anuradha, his great-uncle, and makes it the capital. " Since it had served as dwelling for two Anuradhas it was called Anuradhapura, and also because it was founded under the constellation Anuradha." The town was then of some size, for we read that five hundred low-caste *chandalas* were required to clean the streets. This first king of Anuradhapura, Pandukhabhaya, built the Abhaya-wewa, or Basawak-kulam, and settled the Yakkhas, as well as his Sinhalese, in the capital. Dēvānampiya-Tissa reigned 247–207 B.C., and in 245 B.C. Mahinda, son of the Emperor Asoka, came from India and converted the Sinhalese to Buddhism. The ruins of Anuradhapura are for the most part ecclesiastical in character, and represent the efforts of succeeding kings to glorify the gentle faith by building monasteries for the priesthood and shrines for the sacred relics of the Buddha. In the 5th century A.D. the parricide Kassapa moved the capital to the wonder fortress of Sigiriya, but with this one exception Anuradhapura was the seat of government for some twelve centuries. It saw the Sinhalese race in its prime. Great heroes adorned the historic page, and the legacy they left of the great irrigation works and mighty dagabas tells of a civilisation of which any race would be proud.

In the 8th century A.D. the capital was moved farther inland to Polonnaruwa. Repeated invasions by hordes of treasure-seeking Tamils from Southern India, and the ravages of malaria, had gradually undermined the strength of the Lion Race, until it could no longer defend its ancient city of the plains. But one great figure appears to stem the tide of ruin and decay. Parakrama Bahu the Great in the 12th century A.D. managed to unite the island under one ruler, and even carried the Sinhalese arms with success to India and Pegu. The Sinhalese kings married often with the royal house of Madura ; hence in time they became more Tamil than Sinhalese. Polonnaruwa was the creation of Parakrama Bahu I and his immediate successors, and the ruins express in no uncertain terms their mixed ancestry and their attempt to glorify both the Hindu and Buddhist faiths. To quote Major Henriquez in his *Ceylon Past and Present* :

> Anuradhapura is the expression of an exuberant culture in the vigour of youth, while Polonnaruwa is the last effort of its decay. Anuradhapura is essentially Buddhist and Sinhalese ; Polonnaruwa is the work of hired foreign architects—and Hindu architects at that.

In A.D. 1310 Polonnaruwa in its turn was finally abandoned for Yapahuwa, Dambadeniya, and the security of the hills. The ancient capitals were left to the invader and the jungle. Vegetation covered the shrines, and until last century, when the British began the work of restoration, the great tanks were in disrepair and the dagabas the home of bear and leopard. The Archæological Department has more than justified its existence and still has extensive reserves. Much of the work taken over by the Sinhalese themselves can best be described as merciless. The addition of cheap metal lamps and modern drainpipes has not improved the shrines of Anuradhapura, and one can but blush for these products of Western utility in such a setting.

A word or so of explanation of the chief features of the ruins may be advisable here.

TANKS

Beyond Dambulla, some fifty miles north of Kandy, the traveller will notice many lotus-covered lakes of great beauty. These we desecrate with the dreadful name of "tank." (Sinhalese, *wewa*; Tamil, *kulam.*) Since the rainfall of the northern plains is concentrated within the four months October to January, it is necessary to store the precious water for the remainder of the year. A bund or bank of earth is thrown across a valley, which thus collects the water from the neighbouring higher land. The supply for irrigation and domestic purposes is controlled by sluices, and spills at a lower level than the bunds allow for the escape of surplus water in time of flood. On the security of the tank depends the welfare of the village, for shortage of water means less for cultivation purposes and thus less food. Many of the great tanks of Anuradhapura have bunds several miles in length and cover an area of thousands of acres. Much of the water in the town still comes by a fifty-mile channel from the great reservoir of Kalawewa, which is well worth a short detour of

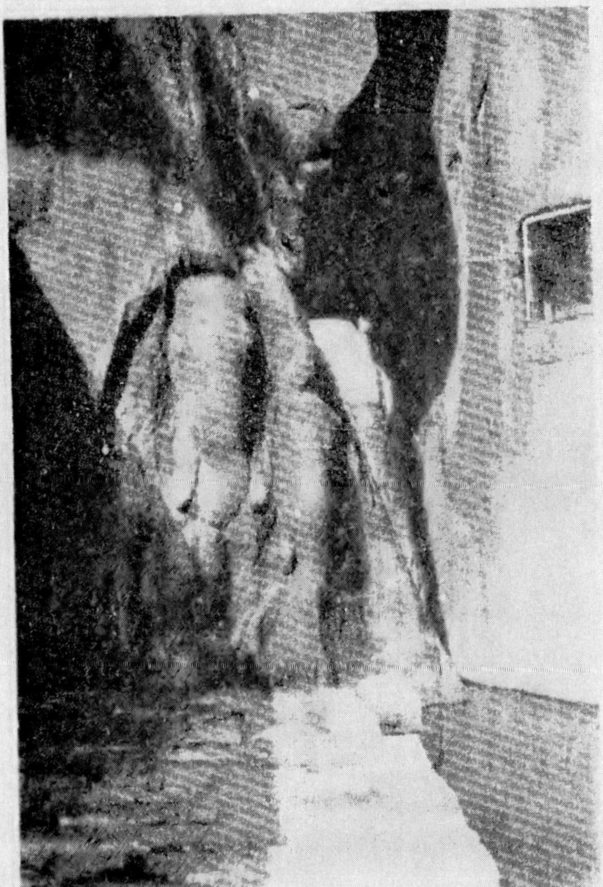

CARVED ELEPHANTS AT ISSURUMUNIYA, ANURADHAPURA

twelve miles as the visitor passes through the village of Kekirawa.

DAGABAS

A dagaba or thupa is a bell-shaped mound of brick and earth sometimes poised on three cylindrical basal ledges, intended for the perambulations of the pious. The dome is surmounted with a square brick tee ornamented with the sun and other demon scarers in relief. Above this tee rises a tapering spire from a cylindrical base topped by a gilded finial. The dagaba is usually surrounded by a paved courtyard within a retaining wall. In the courtyard may be a relic house, statues of the Buddha or of kings, flower altars, a Bo-tree and, as at the Thuparama in Anuradhapura, sundry rows of concentric pillars whose function has been a matter of controversy between archæologists. In the upper part of the dome of the dagaba is a chamber containing a relic of the Buddha or some other saint. The whole of the fabric was plastered and whitened with *chunam*, and the shimmering white and gold mass, often two or three hundred feet in height, was a wonderful sight against the clear blue of the tropic sky.

VIHARE

Great areas of the Buried Cities were covered with monasteries or *vihares*. The city of Anuradhapura was overrun by the yellow robes of the priesthood, and everywhere one comes across remains of their dwelling-places. Mahinda and his disciples lived the life of ascetics in the caves of Mihintale, but, as the priesthood increased, great buildings arose within Anuradhapura. A moonstone and guard stones form part of the entrance. The former is a semi-circular stone doorstep carved with auspicious beasts such as lions, bulls, elephants, etc. The guard stones stand on each side of the steps and usually carry the figure of a naga, also a protector from evil. The stelæ at the side of these naga stones are often of great beauty.

THE CHIEF RUINS OF ANURADHAPURA

1. Brazen Palace.
2. Bo-tree.
3. Ruwanweli Dagaba (Maha Thupa).
4. Selacetiya.
5. Thuparama Dagaba.
6. Tooth Temple (Smithers').
7. Buddhist Railing.
8. Jetawanarama Dagaba (Eastern).
9. Twin Ponds (Kuttam Pokunas).
10. Abhayagiri Dagaba (Northern).
11. Queen's Pavilion.
12. Ratanapāsāda.
13. Stone Canoe.
14. Duttha Gamini's Tomb.
15. Lankarama Dagaba.
16. Dakkhini Vihare (Elara's Tomb).
17. Western Monasteries.
18. Issurumuniya.
19. Vessagiri.
20. Mirisveti Dagaba.

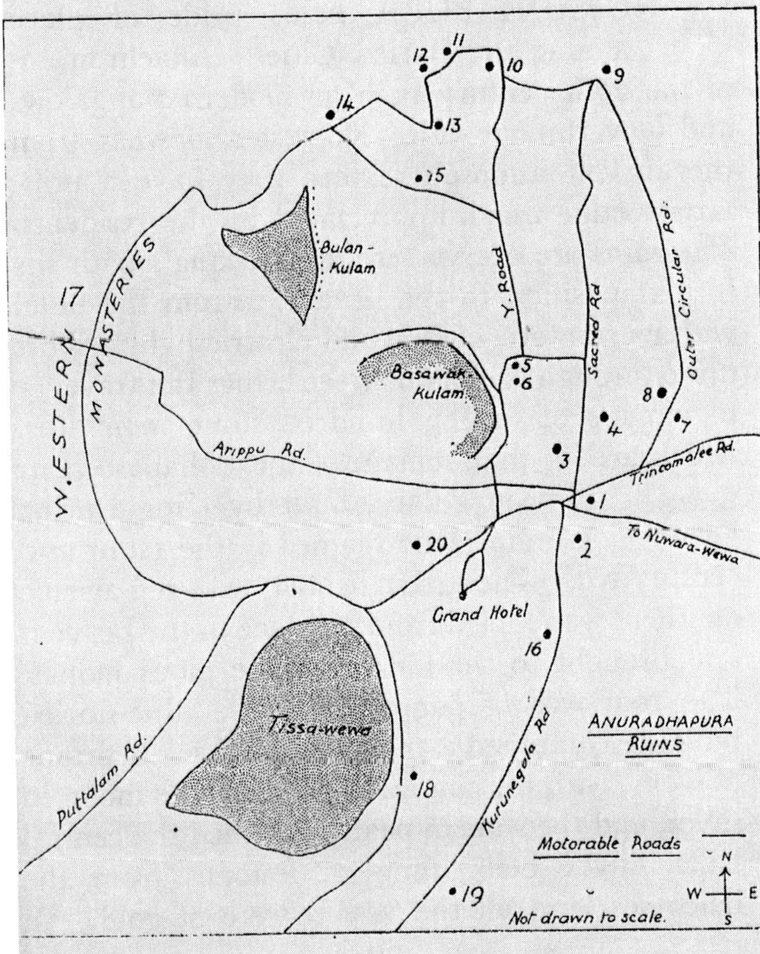

ANURADHAPURA

ANURADHAPURA holds pride of place among the Buried Cities. Anachronisms of the 20th century such as modern bungalows and Government offices detract somewhat from the ancient atmosphere, but they have a utilitarian value much appreciated by the residents. The ruins are everywhere, and a king's bath sits in juxtaposition to the bazaar. From the hotel with its comforts of fans and electric light a short drive through the main street brings the traveller to a mass of sixteen hundred stone monoliths, which are all that remain of the Lohapasada or

Brazen Palace.

Brazen Palace, built by King Duttha Gamini, who reigned in the 1st or 2nd century B.C. The design, drawn with red arsenic on linen, was copied from a palace in the heavens and brought to the king by some pious monks. The roof was of copper, and the nine-storied building contained a thousand rooms. A throne of ivory, with the sun inlaid in gold, the moon in silver, and the stars in pearls, adorned the central hall. Silver bells hung in festoons from the balconies, and all the vessels were of gold. In the reign of Duttha Gamini's successor the great monastery caught fire and was rebuilt to a height of seven stories. It suffered much at the hands of treasure-seeking Tamils and was razed to the ground by the apostate king Maha Sena (3rd century A.D.), who used the materials to enrich the Abhayagiri establishment.

Bo-tree.

Near the Brazen Palace stands the oldest authentic tree in the world, planted here, in the Mahamegha Garden, well over two thousand years ago. The right branch of the tree under which Buddha attained to Nirvana miraculously severed itself from the parent stem. The Emperor Asoka enclosed it in a golden vase and despatched it by his daughter, the nun Sanghamitta, as a gift to Dēvānampiya-Tissa, king of Ceylon 247–207 B.C. King Tissa waded neck deep in the sea to receive it and carried it amid pomp and ceremony to his capital of Anuradhapura. When it was planted the roots grew over and enclosed the vase and a miraculous rain fell for seven days. From its first perfect fruit sprang eight shoots, ancestors of the Bo-trees at the Thuparama, Issurumuniya, and elsewhere. Succeeding kings loved to enrich the surroundings of the sacred tree. There is still sap in the ancient veins, and the yearly crop of leaves is treasured by the yellow-robed guardians who see to it that special earth surrounds the holy stem.

The Sacred Road leads past the Ruwanweli Dagaba, built by Duttha Gamini. The life of this king is so intermingled with the great ruins of Anuradhapura that a few historical facts about him may be of interest. Gamini Abhaya was born in the south of the island. The so-called King's Country, of which Anuradhapura was the centre, was in the hands of the Tamil invaders, ruled by one Elara, whose justice to friend and foe is found worthy of comment even in the Buddhist chronicles. As a lad, Gamini was somewhat unruly. His great desire was to reconquer the kingdom, and when his father refused to allow him to march against the invaders, he sent his cautious parent a piece of female jewellery and earned for himself the prefix of Duttha, the Disobedient. He collected round him a band of heroes, and on his father's death began his military career with a successful campaign against his only brother, from whom he captured his famous elephant Kandula. The brothers were reconciled, and Duttha Gamini was free to turn his attention to the Tamils. He met with varying success, but fought his way eventually to the gates of Anuradhapura, where he on Kandula and Elara on another elephant decided the issue in single combat. The Tamil was slain, but the Sinhalese king buried him with honour and made a decree that even royalty should dismount and

Duttha Gamini, 1st or 2nd century B.C.

RUWANWELI DAGABA (MAHA THUPA), 1931,
ANURADHAPURA

silence its music as it passed the tomb. The mound known locally as Elara's Tomb has been declared by archæologists to be the Dakkhini Vihare, and the grave of the Tamil king is to them still unknown. A tale was told me of a Sinhalese chief who fled from his enemies within living memory past this mound. At the risk of his life, for he had no time to spare, he dismounted and walked past what to him at least was Elara's tomb, obeying the behest of Duttha Gamini. Firmly seated on the throne of his fathers, this king began his career as an architect. On a gold plate hidden in a chest in the palace he found a prophecy that he should build the Ruwanweli or Great Dagaba on a site in the Mahamegha Garden pointed out by Mahinda to King Dēvānampiya-Tissa. Tissa erected a stone pillar with the prophecy engraved thereon on the spot.

Elara's Tomb.

Ruwanweli Dagaba.

Miraculous deposits of copper, silver and jewels occurred all over the island, and since Duttha Gamini wished to acquire all the merit for the work, he decreed that the builders should be paid for their labours as at the building of the Brazen Palace. Heaps of clothing, gold, and food were placed at the city gates for this purpose. Great elephants, their feet bound with leather, trod the foundations, and the boundary of the mighty shrine was traced by a high official with a turning-staff of silver tied to a post of gold. Special "fat-coloured" stone imported from India formed the walls of the relic chamber, which was in the upper part of the dome. In this chamber was a Bo-tree with a silver stem and leaves and fruit of gold and jewels, a canopy festooned with pearls, golden Buddhas on thrones, a magnificent couch for the relics, and other riches without number. Before the shrine was completed Duttha Gamini fell sick. He sent for his brother Saddha-Tissa, who covered the dagaba with a white cloth and erected a temporary spire of bamboo. The dying king was then carried to a spot from which he could see both the Ruwanweli and the Brazen Palace, and died gazing at these, the greatest of his works. Saddha-Tissa completed and probably much enlarged the dagaba, adding a frieze of elephant heads which seem to have disappeared in the present restoration. Later kings built the altars, paved the courtyard, and erected the outer elephant wall. In the courtyard stands a stone statue against a pillar with hands raised in adoration of the shrine. This is King Batiya-Tissa (19 B.C.–A.D. 9), who once covered the dome with a paste of red lead into which he stuck innumerable flowers which were kept fresh by water raised from the Abhaya-wewa by machinery. The statue is much weathered and was found in three pieces. It was carefully restored and erected on the original site. A small cavity below the girdle probably contained treasure which doubtless went the way of all the riches of Anuradhapura. We read of repairs to the Ruwanweli being carried out by later kings, and Parakrama Bahu I in the 12th century A.D. completely restored the building, which had suffered much at the hands of marauding Tamils. The present restoration was undertaken by an energetic young monk in 1873 and is still progressing. The shape of the present dome does not compare very favourably with the original as depicted in Smithers' drawings. Duttha Gamini called together his master builders, five hundred in number, and demanded of them what the shape was to be. One called for a golden bowl of water, and, raising a few drops in his hand he let them fall on the surface of the remainder. A great bubble appeared which was taken as a model. The sand used in the construction was crushed and sifted to prevent the growth of vegetation. Among the modern brickwork recently completed I notice shrubs which have already started the cycle of decay.

Selacetiya.

On the other side of the Sacred Road opposite the Ruwanweli, a short walk takes one to the Selacetiya, a dagaba of peculiar sanctity, being on a site visited by four Buddhas. It was built by Saddha-Tissa, brother and successor of Duttha Gamini, to enshrine a tooth of each of the priests Kujjatissa and Kyaggatissa, personal attendants of Gautama Buddha. The dagaba is of brick with a retaining-wall faced with stone and occupies a very beautiful setting.

Basawak-kulam (Abhaya-wewa).

A bend in the Sacred Road towards a distant tank brings one to the most sacred spot in Anuradhapura. The Basawak-kulam or Abhaya-wewa is the earliest authentic irrigation work in the whole island. It was constructed by Pandukhabhaya, who made Anuradhapura the capital in the 5th century B.C. On its shores stands the oldest known building in India and Ceylon, the Thuparama Dagaba.

Thuparama Dagaba.

It was erected probably in 244 B.C. by Dēvānampiya-Tissa to contain the right collar-bone of the Buddha, which, with his alms-bowl, was the first of the relics sent to the newly-converted Sinhalese by the Emperor Asoka. The relic chamber in the upper portion of the dome was enriched with gold and jewels, and the collar-bone placed in it by King Tissa under the personal supervision of Mahinda, the apostle of Buddhism. Succeeding kings enriched the Thuparama, and one of them made for it a cover of gold with bands of silver, which very soon became the property of the Tamil invaders. In the 12th century A.D. Parakrama Bahu I found the dagaba a jungle-covered mound and restored

THUPARAMA DAGABA, ANURADHAPURA

it. It was again repaired by Parakrama Bahu II, but was in ruins when Sir Emerson Tennent visited Anuradhapura last century. The four concentric rows of stone pillars with carved capitals carried festoons of lamps, and the inner ones appear to have supported some kind of superstructure such as a roof. Many fragments of relic cases were found during the restoration and placed in the Colombo Museum. Repairs have been faithfully carried out, and the Thuparama to-day is a thing of architectural and æsthetic beauty. On the relative proportions of the component parts depends the beauty of a dagaba, and the ugly Lankarama near by makes one appreciate the perfect Thuparama. Round the latter is very holy ground, for the ashes of Mahinda and of his sister Sanghamitta, children of the Emperor Asoka and founders of Buddhism in Ceylon, were buried near by.

As one approaches the Thuparama from the Residency various ruined monasteries offer their beautifully carved guard stones and monoliths to the visitor. Here is the Nandana Garden, or Grove of Light, where Mahinda preached the teachings of Buddha and founded the home of the orthodox faith. The Nandana and Mahamegha Gardens extended from the Basawakkulam to the river, and in this area the most sacred of the shrines are to be found. Nestling under the old red wall of the Thuparama, within the shade of its ancient Bo-tree, are a series of monoliths with carved capitals, part of a two-roomed building which had at one time an underground secret chamber. Smithers identifies this as the Temple of the Tooth, but other experts disagree. Until a building having better claims comes to light I propose to give the historical facts of the relic in connection with these ruins which, being in the most sacred spot of the city, appear to me to have been constructed for a particularly holy purpose. Early in the 4th century A.D. (Codrington places it about A.D. 340) the right eye-tooth of Buddha was brought to King Kitsiri Maiwan (Siri Méghavanna) in Anuradhapura by a princess of Kalinga. Her royal father, besieged in his city of Dantapura, had feared for the fate of the Tooth at the hands of his foes. The waving of a red flag from the city walls was a sign that all was lost, and the princess with the Tooth hidden in her hair fled to Ceylon. She was received with all honour by the Sinhalese king, who built a temple for the sacred relic and instituted the annual *perahera* which, during the August moon, still takes its stately way through the streets of Kandy. The owner of the Tooth and the Bowl became the virtual ruler of the land, so great a hold did they take on the minds of the people. The guardian priests in time of invasion fled through the jungles with their holy burden,

Temple of the Tooth (Smithers).

but the Tamils on one occasion carried the Tooth to India. It was retrieved later, and to the Portuguese we must attribute its final destruction. In the 16th century A.D. this "idol of the heathen" was ground to powder and publicly burnt by the zealous Bishop of Goa. The relic in the Dalada Maligawa at Kandy is but a substitute, but in the eyes of the faithful the Tooth is indestructible, and the measure of its worship from all over the Buddhist world is in no way diminished.

RUINS ON THE OUTER CIRCULAR ROAD

The motorist who desires an evening trip round the Outer Circular Road will be well advised to start at the Tissa end, otherwise he will have the sun in his eyes the whole way. In the morning one leaves the hotel, and after a short drive through the Bazaar and down the Trincomalee Road takes a well-marked turning north. A

Buddhist Railing.

Buddhist railing appears on the right. It will be recognised as a favourite decoration for the tees of the great dagabas, the largest of which rears its jungle-covered dome with brick tee and ruined spire on the left. The energetic can climb to the top of the spire, where a wonderful vista of tank and jungle awaits them. There are well over two hundred feet of very roug going to be negotiated, but this is the easiest dagaba to climb, if climb one must. We have under consideration the Jetawanarama, or Eastern Dagaba, for many years confused with the Abhayagiri. Mr. Neville in 1914 dispelled the local tradition, and the new maps have the ruins marked correctly. At the end of the 3rd century A.D. Maha Sena the apostate was King of the Lion Race in Anuradhapura. For some centuries there had been schism in the Buddhist priesthood, and the Dharmaruchi sect, practising certain heresies, had seceded from the Maha Vihare, the headquarters of the orthodox faith founded by Mahinda, and had established themselves at the Abhayagiri or Northern monastery. Under the influence of Samghamitta, a heretic monk who had been his tutor, Maha Sena dispersed the Maha Vihare and forbade the people to feed its inmates. There was destruction in the Mahamegha and Nandana Gardens. The great Brazen Palace was razed to the ground. and only the assassination of Samghamitta by the queen saved the Thuparama. A rebellion caused the king to see the error of his ways. Anuradhapura, like Paris, was "well worth a 'mass,'" and for a time Maha Sena became an orthodox Buddhist. Seated firmly on the throne, he returned to his evil ways and, in spite of warnings, built the Jetawanarama within the precincts of the Maha Vihare, viz. between the Basawak-

Jetawanar-ama (Eastern) Dagaba.

CARVED STELÆ, JETAWANARAMA (EASTERN) DAGABA,

kulam and the river. It is supposed to have contained a portion of Buddha's girdle. Its riches soon fell to the Tamil invaders, and the structure was much damaged. In the 12th century A.D. Parakrama Bahu I restored it, but with the final abandonment of Anuradhapura it again fell into ruin. Restoration work of the last century has brought to light some beautiful altars and carvings worthy of more than a casual glance, but the jungle still holds sway over the shrine, and further restoration is required in the near future if much is to be preserved. Maha Sena having "acquired much merit and much guilt" is now deified as the god of Minneriya Tank, one of his great irrigation works, which seems to indicate that he was at least mindful of his people's material needs, even if he disagreed with many of them in his religious beliefs.

Twin Ponds—Kuttam Pokunas.

Where the road turns to the west are the Twin Ponds, or Kuttam Pokunas, a ruin of great beauty of design. Anuradhapura is full of bathing-tanks, among which these ponds hold pride of place. Little is known of them, but they are obviously of very ancient date. I hope some day to see them fully restored from Smithers' exquisite drawings.

Following the road, we pass a sedent Buddha and numerous monastic remains until, at the junction of the right-hand branch of the Y-road with the Outer Circular Road, the great mass of the Abhayagiri or Northern Dagaba meets the eye. Round this great shrine has been written much of the early history of Anuradhapura. On this site in the days of Pandukhabhaya (5th century B.C.) stood the Tittharama monastery for Jain ascetics. It was still occupied by this sect when Wattha Gamini Abhaya, nephew of the great Duttha Gamini, began to reign at the beginning of the 2nd century B.C. This king had a Tamil invasion to deal with, and was defeated in a great battle outside the northern gate of the city. As he fled past the Tittharama its high priest, a monk Giri, mocked the royal fugitive, and Wattha Gamini made a vow to destroy the monastery and replace it with a Buddhist community, should he ever recover his throne. The next fifteen years he spent in exile, fed by the priesthood and living in caves and jungles. Dambulla caves became his refuge for a time, and he founded the temple there. His crowning misfortune was to lose the Bowl relic, which the Tamils carried off to India. Wattha Gamini Abhaya, however, came back to the ancient city of his fathers, expelled the invader, and proceeded to fulfil his vow. The Tittharama was destroyed and the community dispersed. On the site rose the Abhayagiri, so called after the king and the monk Giri. In the 2nd century A.D. Gaja Bahu invaded India,

Abhayagiri (Northern) Dagaba.

ABHAYAGIRI (NORTHERN DAGABA), ANURADHAPURA

retrieved the Bowl relic, and restored and enlarged the Abhayagiri. The Chinaman Fa-Hien, who visited Anuradhapura early in the 5th century A.D., left a record of his visit. He calls the great dagaba the "Mountain without Fear" and states that 5,000 monks formed its community. A wonderful blue image of Buddha is mentioned whose hair was composed of sapphires. The Tooth relic, after its arrival, was carried once a year in *perahera* to the Abhayagiri from its temple. There is no doubt that this was the most important monastery in Anuradhapura at the time and became the headquarters of the heretical Dharmaruchi sect which seceded from the Maha Vihare. The shrine was sacked again and again by treasure-seeking Tamils, and Parakrama Bahu I restored it in the 12th century A.D. When the Sinhalese could no longer defend the city the communities dispersed, and the shrines were left to the invader and the jungle. To-day the Abhayagiri is an enormous jungle-covered mound whose slopes offer shelters to troops of monkeys. The heavy *talus* of brick and earth, fallen from the upper slopes of the dome, hides some beautiful carving. The auspicious beasts which adorned the altars push their heads here and there through the débris, and would repay excavation from their jungle tomb. The heretic king Maha Sena used all the materials of the Brazen Palace to enrich this monastery, and enough remains to give the visitor some idea of its past glories. The dome and spire of the dagaba is a pleasing landmark as one approaches Anuradhapura along the Jaffna Road.

Queen's Pavilion.

The next ruin of importance, the Queen's Pavilion, recalls Wattha Gamini Abhaya and his vow. In his flight he took with him his first and second queens, his son and his nephew. The car was overladen and could make but slow progress. The second queen, the beautiful Somadevi, was put down at her own request, and with a portion of the Crown jewels hid in a thicket. She fell to the lot of a Tamil chief who was so enamoured of her beauty that he took her back to India. Fifteen years later her lawful spouse retrieved his captive queen and, in memory of her sacrifice, erected in her honour the Manisomarama monastery on the spot on which she left the car. One likes to think that Somadevi has the most beautiful moonstone in Anuradhapura for a memorial.

Ratana-pāsāda.

Adjoining the Queen's Pavilion is the Ratana-pāsāda, sometimes called the Elephant Stables and the Jewel Palace. It was identified by Mr. Hocart when Government Archæologist as the monastery built by Kanittha Tissa in the 2nd century A.D. This king was so pleased with a monk Mahanaga that "he built for him in splendid fashion the Ratana-pāsāda in the Abhayagiri." At the end of

GUARD STONE, RATANAPĀSĀDA, ANURADHAPURA

the 8th century A.D., Mahinda II rebuilt the "superb many storeyed Ratanapāsāda," and presented to it a golden image of Buddha. The restoration has been well done and the stone-work is very fine indeed. The huge monoliths are a special feature, and the beautiful guard stone, over four feet in height, is a very fine specimen of early carving.

Canopy. Sedent Buddha. Stone Canoe.

On the Loop of the Outer Circular Road is a beautiful stone canopy restored by Mr. S. M. Burrows, within a few yards of which sits a Buddha. This particular statue is a great favourite of mine. His expression is never the same for two days at a time. From complacent retrospection in the sunset comes almost a Mona Lisa smile as the sunlight plays across his stone features. During the roar of the wet monsoon he gives one the impression that the world is a very hard place for everybody.

At the corner of the Loop is an enormous stone canoe which once contained the rice for the monks' refectory. There is a much finer specimen on the hill of Mihintale.

Tomb of Duttha Gamini.

Where the left-hand branch of the Y-road joins the Outer Circular Road stands a brick ruin in a very dilapidated condition. In this travesty of a tomb are supposed to rest the ashes of the greatest hero of the Lion Race, Duttha Gamini. One's memory travels automatically to the sepulchres of the Pharaohs, to the beautiful tombs of European kings of the Middle Ages, and comes back to this brick ruin with a feeling of something lacking of respect. Renowned as he was for his military prowess, his architectural skill and his piety, we can but hope that Duttha Gamini lies elsewhere in a more fitting setting.

A short drive down the Y-road brings one to the Lankarama Dagaba, attributed to our old

Lankarama Dagaba.

friend Wattha Gamini Abhaya of the 1st to 2nd century B.C. The rows of concentric stone pillars remind one of the Thuparama, but the dagaba has not the beautiful lines of the older shrine. It shared the vicissitudes of history in company with the other ruins of Anuradhapura, and has been completely restored.

The Outer Circular Road goes on through innumerable monasteries, which seem to indicate

Western Monasteries.

in no uncertain terms that the city was overrun with the priesthood. These ruins are all of similar design. The stonework is beautiful, and the almost complete absence of carving denotes a very early period. The restoration was carried out by Mr. H. C. P. Bell, of whose genius we have further proof at Sigiriya.

RUINS BELOW TISSA-WEWA

The great tank Tissa was constructed by King Dēvānampiya Tissa in the 3rd century B.C. The

ISSURUMUNIYA, ROCK TEMPLE AND DAGABA,
ANURADHAPURA

bund, which now carries a motorable road, is over two miles in length and, according to Parker, is so well built that with reasonable care it will last for ever. The skeleton of a water-tank was added by the Public Works Department in 1931, and I am glad to say that the cloud of language with which I greeted its appearance was sufficient to turn it green. Among the great rain-trees below the *bund* are numerous ruins. Baths and carved stones occur frequently, and one comes

Issuru-muniya. eventually to the Issurumuniya rock temple and dagaba, which is one of the gems of Anuradhapura. When the Bo-tree was planted by King Tissa in the Mahamegha Garden the Prince Arittha and five hundred of his followers expressed a desire to lead a monastic life. The king built for them the Issurumuniya and constructed at the same time the nearby

Vessagiri. Vessagiri, which was probably a nunnery. Kassapa of Sigiriya, in the 6th century A.D., endeavoured to expiate his sin by rebuilding and enlarging these two settlements. He gave his own name and that of his two daughters, Bodhi and Uppalavanna, to the monastery. Issurumuniya suffered at the hands of the Tamils and finds no place in Smithers' survey of the ruins. Its restoration was, I believe, undertaken by a monk who for many years worked alone or with such casual help as he could persuade the villagers to give him. The shrine is now completely restored. The white dagaba among the old black rocks across the bathing-pool is really lovely, and the carved elephants, probably 4th-century work, offer a pleasing early-morning study to the photographer. One can but deplore the hideous red-brick building and modern belfry which have been added. The dignity and subdued colouring of the ancient Bo-tree cause one to blush for the lamps and other anachronisms of our so-called civilisation, but from the bund it is possible to avoid all this. The shrine then falls into its proper setting of palms and paddy fields, with a glimpse of the hill of Mihintale in the background.

Mirisveti Dagaba.

Near the Jail and within a few minutes' walk of the Grand Hotel is the Mirisveti Dagaba, which derives its name from Miris-wetiya, meaning literally *chilli-sambal.* It was built in the 1st or 2nd century B.C. by Duttha Gamini in expiation of a broken vow. Having concluded his successful campaign against the Tamils with the slaying of Elara at the city gate, the Sinhalese king proceeded to celebrate his return to the capital of his fathers with a water festival in Tissa-wewa. His spear, which contained a relic, was set up by the royal guard on a spot near the tank, together with a heap of riches presented to the conqueror by his courtiers. At the end of the day it was found impossible to

WESTERN ALTAR, MIRISVEṬI DAGABA, ANURADHAPURA

move the spear. As a lad Duttha Gamini had made a vow to share all his food with the monks. He remembered that he had that morning inadvertently eaten some chillies without giving any to the brethren. As a penance he built over the spear the Mirisveti Dagaba, and founded there a monastery which extended to the shores of the Basawak-kulam. It was completed within three years. In the 2nd century A.D., Gaja Bahu I re-coated the dome of the dagaba, and the retaining wall was built later. Parakrama Bahu I found it in ruins and restored it, but when Sir Emerson Tennent visited Anuradhapura last century he described the Mirisveti as "A mere barrow of earth overrun with jungle." A heavy talus completely obscured the basal cylinders. The jungle was cleared, and under the talus on the western side was discovered one of the gems of Buddhist architecture, the finest altar in Anuradhapura. At the cardinal points of the great dagabas of this ancient capital one finds these altars or wāhālkadas as they are called. Smithers describes them as frontispieces, but they appear to be more of the nature of ornamental backgrounds. There is usually a relic-chamber in the rear portion of the fabric, and the decoration of the front and sides consists of rows of auspicious beasts and other demon scarers. At the sides of the altar stelæ are placed. Those at the Mirisveti are 17½ feet in height and are carved throughout their whole length. For many years this western altar at the Mirisveti was protected from the elements by the débris with which it was covered. The stone used in its construction is a very hard granite, and the carvings are in an excellent state of preservation.

Nuwara-wewa.

As one enters Anuradhapura along the Matale Road an enormous green bank appears on the left. This is the bund of Nuwara-wewa, the City Tank, and on the top of the bund is a motorable road some three miles in length. Parker worked on the Anuradhapura tanks for some time, and is an authority on dates where their construction is concerned. He attributes Nuwara-wewa to the early part of the 1st century B.C. There is a possibility that it was built by Wattha Gamini Abhaya. Below the bund are sundry ruins, but the *pièce de résistance* is the sunsets with the hills of Mihintale and Ritigala reflected across the immense stretch of waters. The tourist will be delighted too with the moonlight pictures, and the view of the great dagabas of the city across the paddy fields is very fine indeed. I advise the pedestrian out for a nocturnal ramble to take a stout stick with which to deal with any snakes that may be abroad. Not every snake is venomous, but it is safer to assume that the reptile is better dead unless it removes itself immediately.

MIHINTALE

EIGHT miles from Anuradhapura on the road to Trincomalee lies the little jungle village of Mihintale, its tiny houses grouped around the foot of the Missaka Mountain. Here is the cradle of Buddhism in Ceylon. The hill of Mihintale, to give it its modern name, is so called after the apostle Mahinda, son of the Emperor Asoka, who in the 3rd century B.C. was despatched by his royal father to King Dēvānampiya-Tissa with the message of the gentle faith. The religion of the Sinhalese before his coming is a matter of conjecture. Jainism is mentioned, and some form of Nature worship existed. On circuit in the northern jungles I have often seen one of our escort of headmen hang a twig across a bough as we entered on a jungle path. This was an offering to a god of the forests, who then protected the party from attacks from wild beasts, etc. There is still a firm belief in devils in the villages. Buddhism immediately took a firm hold on the Lion Race and is still the religion of the majority. The tale of its coming is recorded in great detail in the

Mahawansa. After he had reigned for two years in Anuradhapura, King Tissa, having arranged a water festival for the dwellers in the city, set out with thousands of his followers on a hunting expedition to Mihintale. He was led by an elk-stag up the mountain, and in pursuit of the quarry, came across a band of yellow-robed monks who had appeared from nowhere. Mahinda was at their head, and, as King Tissa was on very friendly terms with the Emperor Asoka, he listened with great joy to the son of his friend. Never had a missionary such a response. The king and all his followers were there and then converted, and the construction of monasteries and shrines for the relics of the Buddha became the daily occupation of the royal convert. On the mountain were constructed numerous rock cells as homes for the ascetics, and in the capital Mahinda received the king's pleasure garden as a home for the faith. Tissa, with two elephants harnessed to a golden plough, marked the boundaries of the lands, which extended over what is now known as the Mahamegha and Nandana Gardens between the Basawak-kulam and the river. The Thuparama and other shrines arose in Anuradhapura, but Mahinda lived on his mountain with periodic visits to the capital. Mihintale was literally covered with shrines and is known in the chronicles as the Cetiya Mountain, *cetiya* meaning shrine. The ruined cells and dagabas testify to the existence of a large community of monks, which probably exceeded 3,000 in number.

The traveller motors to the foot of a flight of steps composed of enormous blocks of granite. There are some 1,080 of these to be negotiated, but the guide leaves them after a flight or so for a rough jungle path on the right. Sundry cave-dwellings catch the eye (when one is not stumbling over tree-roots) and we reach the Lion Bath, so called from a somewhat battered stone lion which forms part of the structure. A stiff climb takes us to the Naga Pokuna or Snake Bath. It is an enormous rock-pool with a huge five-headed cobra sculptured on the far wall. King Tissa is stated to have rested by this Naga Pokuna after he had met Mahinda, so that it was in existence prior to 245 B.C. The view from here is wonderful. The dagabas and tanks of Anuradhapura are clearly visible, and the foreground offers a fine picture of a hill covered with caves.

Lion Bath.

Snake Bath (Naga Pokuna).

We climb next to the Ambatthala platform on which Tissa and Mahinda met. A stone statue of the king marks the spot on which he stood. The statue is much weathered, but shows a royal dignity and should be better protected from the elements. A newly restored white dagaba, the Ambatthala, marks the

Statue of King Tissa.

spot on which Mahinda stood. It was built by Maha Naga early in the 1st century B.C. Local tradition places the ashes of Mahinda inside the dome, but as he was cremated and buried near the Thuparama in Anuradhapura this is probably untrue. The concentric rows of stone pillars which adorn the platform are similar to those at the Thuparama.

Ambatthala Dagaba.

The preaching rock behind the dagaba offers a glimpse of Mahinda's bed, an enormous rock in the distance. Above the platform is the huge brick mass of the Maha Saeya, built in 243 B.C., by King Tissa to enshrine a hair of the Buddha. Its partial restoration was carried out by Mr. Ievers, when Government Agent of the province.

Maha Saeya.

On the highest point of all a mass of débris is all that remains of the Aet or Tusk-elephant Dagaba of very early date.

Aet Dagaba.

Parakrama Bahu I in the 12th century A.D. is stated to have restored over sixty shrines on Mihintale. Thunderstorms are a feature of this district and there is no doubt that the dagabas were often struck by lightning. Attempts at lightning conductors were made as early as the 5th century A.D., but needless to say they were not effective.

Coming down the hill by the granite staircase one passes numerous small mounds which mark the graves of monks. At the half-way house are two enormous stone slabs covered with legible inscriptions in Pali. These are literally "Tables of the Law" on which rules of conduct for the community of priests are inscribed. Just below is the refectory with the finest specimen of a stone canoe that I have ever seen. It was used for rice, as already stated.

" Tables of the Law."

Stone Canoe.

Down the stairway one travels to the village below, where a short walk takes one to the Idikatu or Needles Dagaba, built by Kalakenni Tissa in the 1st century B.C. Parker finds the stone wall surrounding the monastery worthy of comment.

Idikatu (Needles) Dagaba.

Mihintale suffered the fate of Anuradhapura at the hands of the Tamils, whose ruthless destruction of the shrines was repaid with the great riches with which they were embellished. Later kings restored them from time to time, but finally that persistent enemy, the jungle, exerted its sway. A few monks still tend the ruins and bathe in the ancient Naga Pokuna. The June moon ushers in the Poson festival, which is held in honour of Mahinda. Mihintale then comes to life. The roads swarm with pilgrims, and on the old old stairway one meets devotees of the gentle faith, their hands full of the blue lotus and other blossoms. Myriads of tiny lamps adorn the shrines, and the altars are rich with the scent of flowers, the universal offering.

POLONNARUWA

THE road to Polonnaruwa from Habarane offers a glimpse of the great tank of Minneriya, one of the most beautiful in the island. A short détour takes one to the circuit bungalow, whence a walk of a mile produces some old stone statues on the *bund*. Minneriya was the work of Maha Sena I, the heretic king who, in the 3rd century A.D., destroyed the Maha Vihare in Anuradhapura. In the little jungle village he is now worshipped as the god of the tank.

Minneriya.

Polonnaruwa, the ancient Pulatthi-nagara of the chronicles, became the capital at the end of the 8th century A.D. It had been an important settlement before this date and offered a fitting sanctuary for the seat of government when Anuradhapura could no longer be defended from the Tamil. The new city reached its zenith under Parakrama Bahu I in the 12th century A.D. For many years Sinhalese history had been a sorry tale of foreign invasion and internal strife. Petty kings wasted their energies in the assassina-

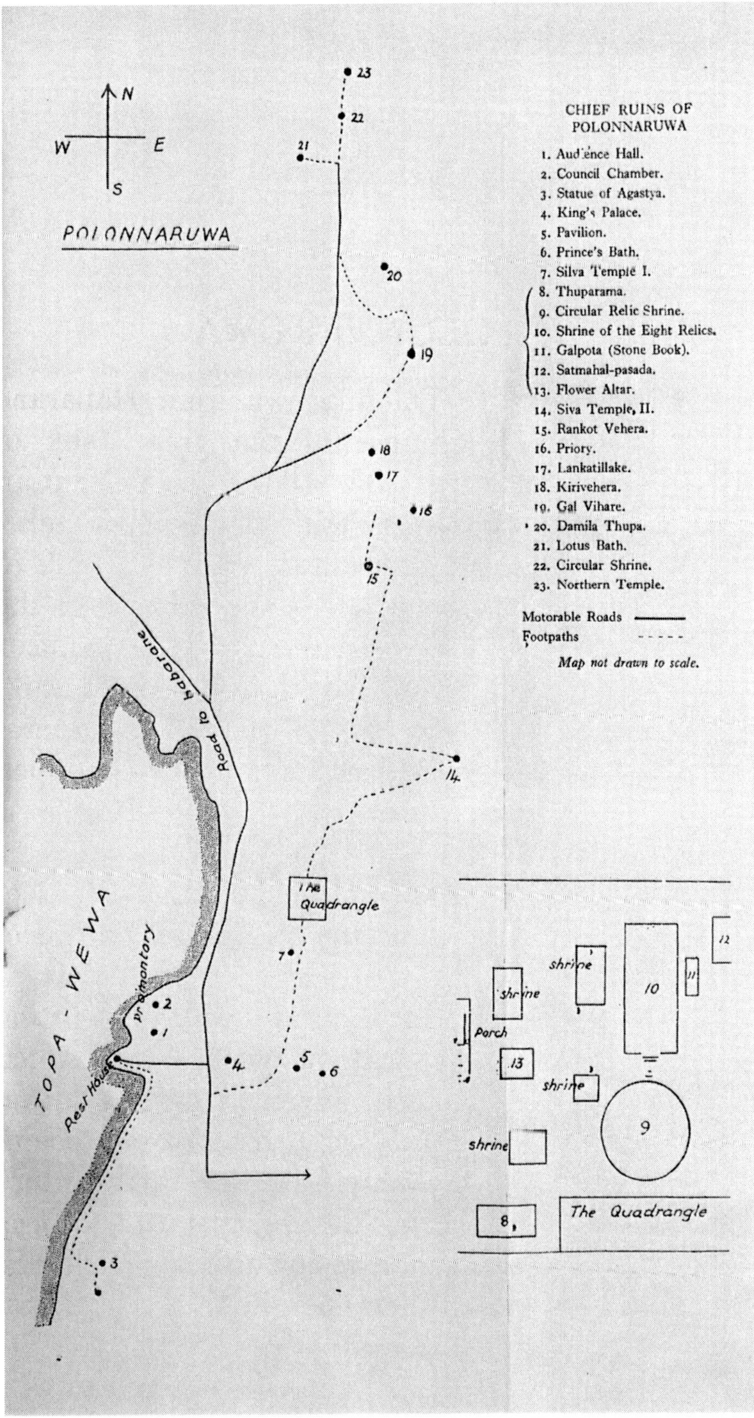
N
W
E
S
POLONNARUWA
CHIEF RUINS OF POLONNARUWA
1. Audience Hall.
2. Council Chamber.
3. Statue of Agastya.
4. King's Palace.
5. Pavilion.
6. Prince's Bath.
7. Silva Temple I.
8. Thuparama.
9. Circular Relic Shrine.
10. Shrine of the Eight Relics.
11. Galpota (Stone Book).
12. Satmahal-pasada.
13. Flower Altar.
14. Siva Temple, II.
15. Rankot Vehera.
16. Priory.
17. Lankatillake.
18. Kirivehera.
19. Gal Vihare.
20. Damila Thupa.
21. Lotus Bath.
22. Circular Shrine.
23. Northern Temple.
Motorable Roads
Footpaths
Map not drawn to scale.
Road to Habarane
TOPA-WEWA
promontory
Rest House
The Quadrangle
shrine
shrine
shrine
shrine
Porch
The Quadrangle

tion of their immediate neighbours, and no combined resistance to the invader was possible. The Lion Race, degenerate as it had become, could yet produce one great figure, and Parakrama Bahu the Great was worthy of the old heroes from whom he was descended. The young princeling from the sub-kingdom of Ruhuna showed himself wise and sagacious at a very early age. He conceived the idea of a united Ceylon under himself as sole monarch, and set out to achieve his aim with any methods that suggested themselves to his very fertile brain. It was an age of cruelty and bloodshed, and Parakrama Bahu, with more than his share of the first commodity, saw to it that there was plenty of the second. A visit to his kinsman ruling in Polonnaruwa made it possible for him to found a spy system among the subjects of his trusting host. The greatest warrior and statesman of his time finally spread his " umbrella of dominion " over the whole island, and even carried his arms with success against the King of Pegu and into the Chola country of Southern India. A standing army of well-trained mercenaries and a civil service maintained law and order throughout the king's dominions, and we read that a woman could pass from one end of the land to the other with a rich jewel, and not be molested. In his long reign of thirty-three years Parakrama Bahu

Parakrama Bahu I. (A.D. 1153-86)

had time for the arts of peace. The great irrigation works were restored, and prosperity followed in their wake. The shrines of Anuradhapura and Mihintale were rebuilt, and the new capital of Polonnaruwa bid fair to rival the old in the richness and dimensions of its shrines. It is a strange medley of architecture, which tells of the civilisation of the Sinhalese in the 12th century A.D. As already stated, frequent intermarriage with the royalty of Madura had finally produced a race of princes more Tamil than Sinhalese. In the great city of Parakrama Bahu, Hindu and Buddhist shrines sit side by side. It was an age of ostentation and over-decoration. The dignity and reserve of the pre-Christian shrines found no place in the work of hired foreign architects who produced the buildings of Polonnaruwa, and Westminster Abbey compares very favourably with the Lankatillake of a later date.

The visitor to the ruins of this medieval capital stays at the Rest House, which occupies a delightful site on the *bund* of Topawewa, a great tank which once formed part of the Sea of Parakrama. At the time of writing there are few crocodiles left, but the bird life is a joy to the ornithologist, and the sunsets are guaranteed to please an artist.

The archæologist will find a good deal of material on the Promontory, a few yards from the Rest House. The Audience Hall and Council

Chamber are those of Nissanka Malla, a king of pure Tamil descent who was son-in-law or nephew to Parakrama Bahu I, and succeeded him after the lapse of a year. An enormous stone lion which formed part of Nissanka Malla's throne was conveyed with great difficulty to the Colombo Museum. This king had a perfect mania for inscriptions, which we find all over the capitals. His literary style was bombastic in the extreme, and many of the shrines which he claims to have constructed suffered only a modicum of restoration at his hands.

Audience Hall. Council Chamber.

A pleasant evening walk of just over a mile along the tank *bund* brings one to the Potgul Vehera. Here is an enormous stone statue cut from the solid rock, which for many years has been taken to represent Parakrama Bahu the Great. Dr. Nell identifies it as the sage Agastya, which is a much more likely supposition. The learned one is intent on the study of an *ola* and has an air of great dignity among his peaceful jungle surroundings.

Potgul Vehera. Statue of Agastya.

Where the road to the Rest House joins the main road a somewhat ugly mass of red brick rears its façade above the old green bank. This is the royal palace, probably of later date than Parakrama Bahu. Round it were pleasure gardens and pavilions. There

King's Palace.

is a pleasing specimen of the latter near by, in close proximity to the Prince's Bath or Kumārapokuna with its spouts of crocodile heads.

Prince's Bath.

A footpath leads to the little Siva Temple I, a shrine in the best Hindu style whose carvings are really lovely.

Siva Temple I.

RUINS IN THE QUADRANGLE

Fifty or sixty years ago the Quadrangle was a mass of jungle. Great trees grew within the shrines and their roots spread ruin and disintegration through the fabric. The undergrowth hid the fallen pillars, and the great stone Buddhas had in many cases left their pedestals. Our busy Archæological Department is to be congratulated on the state of this great enclosure at the present day. The buildings have been restored by experts, and the smooth green turf is an ideal setting for the remains of the old civilisation.

As we enter by the footpath from the Siva Temple I, the huge mass of ornate masonry on the left denotes the Thuparama. This strange building, so essentially Hindu in structure and design, is a Buddhist shrine. It is the only building of any size in the ancient capitals which still possesses a roof, an excellent spot from which to photograph the other ruins

Thuparama.

THE QUADRANGLE FROM THE THUPARAMA, POLONNARUWA

in the Quadrangle. Mr. S. M. Burrows in 1886 cleared the great blocks of fallen masonry which filled the entrance and removed the jungle from the walls. The inner shrine contains sundry Buddhas and a stone slab on which Parakrama Bahu was wont to meditate. The atmosphere is somewhat eerie and one emerges into the sunlight with relief. Near the Thuparama is the gem of the Quadrangle, the Circular Relic Shrine, which was Parakrama Bahu's Temple of the Tooth. Many of the statues of Buddha in the temples of the Quadrangle face towards this shrine which was the most sacred building in the city. The main entrance is a magnificent stone stairway which rises from its moonstone by a series of decorated steps to an upper platform with four sedent Buddhas. The monoliths with carved capitals recall the Thuparama of Anuradhapura, and some of the guard stones on the lower courtyard would not have disgraced the buildings of the old capital. Devotees still light their tiny lamps and lay their flowers before the statues of the Enlightened One.

Circular Relic Shrine.

Opposite the northern stairway of the Circular Shrine is the Shrine of the Eight Relics built by Nissanka Malla. This king is responsible for the enormous Galpota or Stone Book which lies near by. The inscription tells of the ancestry and merits of

Shrine of the Eight Relics.

Nissanka Malla, who appears to have been a marvellous individual in his own estimation. On one inscription we are told that a snake approached the king as he was going to his bath. The monarch pointed out to the reptile its lack of respect, whereupon the poor creature committed suicide for very shame. The Galpota weighs well over twenty tons, and according to the inscription was "brought from the mountain of Saegiri (Mihintale) by the strong men of King Nissanka," some 80 miles.

Stone Book.

The seven-storied shrine is the Satmahalpāsāda. It is Cambodian in design, and doubtless is a monument to Parakrama Bahu's campaign in that country. A staircase on the outside leads to a second storey, and the whole fabric is decorated.

Satmahal-pāsāda.

Near the western porch is the Flower Altar, the work of Nissanka Malla. The carved and twisted pillars are perfect gems and the peculiar stone railing a fitting frame. The lotus theme is everywhere, and we can but think that the king had here a much better memorial than the flowery language with which he decorated his capital.

Flower Altar.

A footpath leads to the Siva Temple II, well worth more than a casual glance by the visitor.

Siva Temple II.

FLOWER ALTAR, THE QUADRANGLE, POLONNARUWA

RUINS IN THE LANKATILLAKE SECTION

The visitor to the Lankatillake has a choice of routes. He can motor in comfort or he can walk by a footpath from the Quadrangle. I would impress on the pedestrian the necessity for a stout walking-stick and a wary eye for snakes, also the inadvisability of sitting down for a rest. There are no leeches in the dry zone, but they have their counterpart in ticks, which have very similar habits where human beings are concerned. Ants, too, are everywhere, and most varieties can be relied on to make their presence felt in a very short space of time and in a painful manner. Wild beasts avoid one for the most part, but a nocturnal visitor would be a congenital idiot to try these unfrequented paths without a rifle.

The Lankatillake is well worth a little energy. The huge brick mass dominates the landscape, and is a strange building for a Buddhist shrine. The interior possesses some peculiar features, and the enormous Buddha at the end is worthy of inspection. The roof, of course, has completely disappeared. This has its advantages, for the remaining traces of mural decoration are clearly visible in the sunlight which penetrates to every corner. The foreign workmen of Parakrama Bahu left their mark both in the design and decoration of the shrine.

Lankatillake.

The plastered dome of the Kirivehera Dagaba sits in complacent ugliness near by. South of the Lankatillake another large dagaba is silhouetted on the horizon. This is the Rankot Dagaba, sometimes called the Ruwanweli, built by Nissanka Malla. The grey monoliths of the Priory between the Rankot Dagaba and the Lankatillake remind the visitor that he is dealing with the same race that created Anuradhapura. For further proof of this let us walk through the jungle to the Gal Vihare, one of the finest things that Ceylon possesses. Parakrama Bahu is stated to have excavated this shrine and left there a fine inscription testifying to his pious works. The Gal Vihare, as its name imples, is a rock temple sacred to Buddha and entirely lacking in the ostentatious trimmings of the 12th century. An enormous sedent figure comes first with a smaller one within the central shrine. The *pièce de résistance* is the standing figure on its lotus throne, which has been identified by some as the favourite disciple Ananda, weeping over the recumbent figure of the Enlightened One who has attained Nirvana. Dr. Nell disagrees with the Ananda theory. The pedestal seems to denote, as he suggests, a Buddha himself, and the expression of sorrow on the features may well be attributed to the elements. The foundation of a wall between the two figures

Kirivehera.

Rankot Dagaba.

Priory.

Gal Vihare.

is clearly visible and they were no doubt originally in separate shrines.

The energetic can walk from the Gal Vihare by a jungle path to join the main road to the Northern Temple. He will pass the enormous mass of the Damila Thupa, so-called because it was constructed by the Tamils.

Damila Thupa.

RUINS IN THE NORTHERN TEMPLE SECTION

The road north from the Lankatillake ends at a notice board which offers the visitor the Lotus Bath at the expense of a short walk. This little gem owes its discovery to Mr. John Still, whose *Jungle Tide* by a real jungle lover has introduced Polonnaruwa to a large public. The bath with its exquisite steps, each a petal of the lotus, has been completely restored. It beggars description, and must be seen to be believed. I have heard rumours of a similar bath a few miles off in the jungle.

Lotus Bath.

A footpath, a continuation of the motorable road, leads past a circular shrine very similar in design to the gem in the Quadrangle. It is much smaller and at best a crude imitation of the other.

Circular Shrine.

The Northern Temple is very like the Lankatillake. There are some beautiful frescoes in the interior, and the carved friezes on the outside walls are a favourite subject with photographers.

Northern Temple.

SIGIRIYA. THE LION ROCK

"THEREUPON the wicked ruler called Kassapa sent forth his groom and his cook. But as he was unable through these to slay his brother, he betook himself through fear to Sinhagiri which is difficult of ascent for human beings. He cleared the land round about, surrounded it with a wall and built a staircase in the form of a lion." So runs the ancient chronicle, and the quotation promises a tale not unworthy of the sagas.

In the 5th century A.D., Dhatu Sena was king of the Sinhalese in the ancient city of Anuradhapura. He had cleared the hated Tamils from the holy places, restored the ravished shrines, and spread law and order over a land which for years had been at the mercy of the invader. His greatest achievement was the great jungle tank of Kalawewa. Dhatu Sena, like all great men, had his enemies. His action in sending traitor nobles and their families to dwell among the lowest caste in the land did not make for popularity with one of the proudest races in the world. The king had two sons, Moggallana by his chief queen, and Kassapa by a queen of inferior caste.

He had also a daughter on whom he lavished all the affection of a strong nature. This daughter was married to Migara, nephew to the king and commander-in-chief of the army. In a fit of jealousy Migara struck his wife, who fled with her bloodstained garments to her royal father. Vengeance for the wrong came quickly. In the absence of Migara his mother was burned alive by the angry king. Kassapa seized his opportunity. Together with Migara supported by the army, he took the capital and imprisoned his father. Moggallana fled to India and Kassapa assumed the kingship. The captive Dhatu Sena was asked for the whereabouts of the royal treasure and, desiring once again to see his friend the monk Mahanama, and his great tank, said that the treasure was hidden at Kalawewa. He was taken through the jungle, and we read that the kindly driver of the cart shared his food with his captive king. Dhatu Sena gave him a writing for Moggallana, asking that in the event of his regaining his father's throne, he would make the carter doorkeeper to his palace. Eighteen years later Moggallana carries out his murdered father's wishes. Meanwhile, Dhatu Sena, having conversed with Mahanama and bathed in Kalawewa, announced that his only treasures were his friend and the great tank. He was dragged back to Anuradhapura, where his unnatural son and nephew walled him up alive.

SIGIRIYA· THE ROCK FROM THE TANK

Kassapa does not seem to have been happy in his stolen honours and, when repeated attempts to assassinate his brother had failed, fear and a guilty conscience drove him to build his impregnable fortress of Sigiriya. Wall after wall round the great rock but served to remind the parricide of that first dreadful wall he built in Anuradhapura, and an orgy of good works and gifts to the priesthood failed to soothe a guilty conscience. For years the master mind toiled at the fortress, and yet, when Moggallana came at last bent on vengeance, Kassapa left his crag and met his brother in the plain. Perhaps the double traitor Migara, who appears as an official of rank at Moggallana's court, may have had something to do with it, or maybe the unhappy king chose to die rather than live with his accusing conscience any longer. During the battle Kassapa's elephant wandered into a marsh, and when the king turned it to find a surer road his followers thought him to be fleeing from the field. Seeing his troops scatter, he killed himself on his elephant, and, like another royal one, " nothing in his life became him like the leaving of it." Moggallana buried his brother with all honour, and removed the seat of government back to Anuradhapura. Sigiriya was given to the priesthood, whose cave dwellings remain to-day in great numbers in the jungle at the foot of the rock. Kassapa left a monument of which a Pharaoh could be proud. Imagine an enormous mass of granite 400 feet in height, with an acre or so on the top, and overhanging on three sides. Conceive the brain which hung a stairway round this crag, built an enormous lion's head on the one platform, and constructed a palace and its attendant baths and reservoirs on the summit. Note the great polished gallery in which four men could walk abreast, the elephant stables, the audience hall, and the thirteen terraces. The frescoes of the "Ladies of Sigiriya" still retain their colours and look as of old towards the temples on the northern hill.

The work of restoration was in the capable hands of Mr. H. C. P. Bell. The tombstones at the foot of the stairway tell their own tale of hardship and death in the war waged against malaria. In spite of great difficulties Mr. Bell slung his workmen from the top of the crag, and those of us who are brave enough to venture beyond the Lion's Jaws, have not only a permanent iron stair, but a handrail as well with which to negotiate the upper slopes. I have been privileged to see Mr. Bell's photographs of the work of restoration, and would state that the modern Sigiriya is almost as much a monument to him as to its original architect.

THE ROCK TEMPLE OF DAMBULLA

DAMBULLA lies forty-five miles north of Kandy on the road to Anuradhapura. The caves offered shelter to Wattha Gamini Abhaya, nephew of Duttha Gamini. Expelled from the capital by the Tamils, the king wandered an exile for fifteen years, when he returned in triumph to build the Abhayagiri Dagaba in the ancient city. He beautified the Dambulla caves, and the work was restored and re-decorated by later kings of the Polonnaruwa period. That inveterate scribbler Nissanka Malla left his mark on the shrine, which was built originally in the 1st century B.C.

The tourist will find awaiting him at the foot of the hill sundry unpleasant people desirous of becoming guides and camera bearers. For this he is in some ways responsible, and indiscriminate tipping in the past has much to answer for. The climb to the caves is steep and lies over bare unshaded rock. The unwary may find himself paying an entrance fee at each of the five sections of the shrine. The second cave is by far the finest. On a wet day the rock is slippery and very dangerous for the traveller whose pedal extremities are shod with rubber. I have in mind a tourist who put his hip out at the top of Dambulla and found the journey down on coolie shoulders, and the subsequent drive back to Kandy and the nearest surgeon, anything but pleasant.

ALUWIHARE

A FEW miles from Matale the Aluwihare caves and temple may tempt the tourist to wander a mile or so from the main road. In the time of Wattha Gamini Abhaya (1st century B.C.) there was much schism in the Buddhist priesthood. The orthodox faith had been handed down orally from Mahinda by the monks of the Maha Vihare in Anuradhapura. The king fearing the effect of the new heresies decreed that the tenets of the faith as preached by Mahinda should be written down and preserved. The writing was done at Aluwihare Temple.

KALAWEWA

THERE have been several references in this book to the tank of Kalawewa which can be reached, as already stated, by a six-mile drive from the village of Kekirawa. The great reservoir has been restored under British rule and fulfils its original functions. One is apt to forget that it formed a part of the old civilisation. Its construction by Dhatu Sena in the 5th century A.D. recalls the story of Sigiriya and the dreadful death of the king at the hands of his son and his nephew. The remains of the old monastery on the *bund* speak of Mahanama and his last interview with his sovereign. Near by too are the ruins of the city of Vijitapura, somewhat confused in the chronicles with a town of the same name near Polonnaruwa. A jungle walk of a mile or so brings one to the colossal Buddha of Awkana.

The *bund* of Kalawewa extends for five or six miles. The motorist at one point crosses the main spill, a dangerous proceeding when there is any quantity of water coming down. I have spent pleasant hours in the little circuit bungalow, which occupies a site near an ugly modern monument.